BECKFORD'S TOWER, BATH

An Illustrated Guide

Jon Millington

A Bath Preservation Trust Museum

Foreword

By Michael Briggs, Chairman, Bath Preservation Trust

Since Bath Preservation Trust became the sole trustee of the Beckford Tower Trust in 1993, there has been a transformation in its fortunes.

In 1995 it was realised that very considerable repairs were necessary to the Tower and we accepted that only with the support of the Heritage Lottery Fund and a public appeal could we achieve this.

The Beckford Tower Trust applied to the Heritage Lottery Fund in 1997 and we were successful in obtaining a grant of £462 500 and raising a sum of approximately £180 000 as matching funding through public appeal, charitable trusts and the resources of the Bath Preservation Trust and Beckford Tower Trust. This enabled us to undertake the restoration of the Tower, the lantern and the Belvidere, the regilding of the lantern, and the refurbishment of the museum on the first floor.

In 1999 we were very glad to grant a long term tenancy of the ground floor to the Landmark Trust, who have created an apartment in the spirit of Beckford.

It has been encouraging to see that William Beckford has attracted a great deal of attention through the extensive press coverage of the Tower restoration project and the exhibition "William Beckford 1760-1844: An Eye for the Magnificent" held in New York and London 2001 / 2002.

We are grateful to Jon Millington for his scholarly update of this guide to Beckford's Tower.

We look forward to welcoming visitors to the restored Beckford's Tower and the museum.

Chronology of William Beckford

1760   September 29. William Beckford born at Soho Square, London.

1764   Later claimed to have been Mozart's pupil.

1766   Or thereabouts. Portrait painted by Andrea Casali.
        (Now in Lennoxlove, Scotland.)

1770   June 21. Death of his father, Alderman Beckford.
        Buried at Fonthill.

1773   Alexander Cozens appointed his drawing master.

1777   June. First visit abroad, to Geneva with his tutor,
        Rev. John Lettice, until November 1778.
        December. Wrote *The Long Story*, published as *The Vision* in 1930.

1779   June. Met William 'Kitty' Courtenay at Powderham Castle,
        Devon, during English tour.
        Winter. Met Louisa, wife of his first cousin Peter Beckford,
        at Fonthill.

1780   Spring. *Biographical Memoirs of Extraordinary Painters* published.
        June. Embarked with Lettice on the Grand Tour until April 1781.
        November. Met Lady Hamilton, wife of Sir William, in Naples.

1781   Or 1782. His overture to the ballet *Phæton* published in Paris.
        February. In Paris for two months on his way back from Italy.
        June. Portrait painted by George Romney.
        (Now in Upton House, Banbury.)
        Coming-of-age and Christmas parties at Fonthill Splendens.

1782   January-August. Wrote *Vathek* in French.
        February-May. Portrait painted by Joshua Reynolds.
        (Now in National Portrait Gallery.)
        April. Performance of his score for Lady Craven's operetta
        Arcadian Pastoral.
        May-November. Second tour to Italy, with retinue including
        John Robert Cozens.

1783   April. *Dreams, Waking Thoughts, and Incidents* suppressed on
        publication.
        May 5. Married Lady Margaret Gordon. Honeymoon in
        Switzerland.

1784   January-March. In Paris. Attended sale of Duc de la Vallière's
        library.
        April. M.P. for Wells.
        May. Their first child stillborn.
        September. Scandal at Powderham Castle.
        October. His name in list of those to be raised to the peerage.

1785   April 9. Birth of elder daughter, Maria Margaret Elizabeth, at
        Fonthill.
        July. In Switzerland, with his wife. He stayed until the end of 1786.

1786   May 14. Birth of younger daughter, Susan Euphemia.
        May 26. Death at Vevey of his wife, 12 days later, aged 23.
        June 7. Unauthorised publication by Henley of *Vathek* in English.

1787   March. First visit to Portugal, until November, then Spain until
        June 1788.
        May 28. Met Gregorio Franchi in Lisbon.

1788   July. In Paris, mostly at rue de Varenne, until August 1789.

1789   August. In Switzerland.

1790   Spring. Commissioned Gothic ruin from James Wyatt.
        October. In Paris until June 1791.

1791   April 30. Death at Florence of Louisa Beckford, aged 35.
        November. In Paris at rue de Grenelle and elsewhere in
        Europe until May 1793.

1793   Autumn. Ordered barrier wall to be built round the Fonthill
        estate.
        November. Second visit to Portugal until October 1795,
        then elsewhere until March 1796.

1794   June 2-13. Visited monasteries of Alcobaça and Batalha in
        Portugal.

1795   Winter. *Modern Novel Writing* published.

1796   Summer. Building of Fonthill Abbey began.
        Bought Gibbon's library for £950.
        Christmas. Grand fête at Fonthill for tenants and workmen.

1797   *Azemia* published.

1798   July 22. Death at Hampstead of his mother, the 'Begum'.
        Buried at Fonthill.
        October. In Portugal until about July 1799.

1799   Autumn. Watercolours of Fonthill Abbey commissioned from
        J. M. W. Turner.

1800   Or thereabouts. Portrait painted by John Hoppner.
        (Now in Salford Art Gallery.)
        December 20-24. Lord Nelson, Sir William and Lady Hamilton
        at Fonthill for Christmas.

1801   May. In Paris at rue St Dominique until May 1803.

1806   December. M.P. for Hindon.

1807   Summer. Moved to Fonthill Abbey and demolished Splendens.

1810   April 26. Susan married the Marquis of Douglas, later 10th
        Duke of Hamilton.

1811   February 18. Birth to Susan of first of his five grandchildren,
        William, later 11th Duke.
        May 15. Margaret eloped with Colonel (later General)
        James Orde.

1812   Building of the Eastern Transept of Fonthill Abbey began.

1814   October-December. Visited Paris.

1818   September 7. Death at Bath of Margaret, aged 33.

1819   February 16. His son-in-law became 10th Duke of Hamilton
        on father's death.
        May-June. Last visit to Paris.
        End of building at Fonthill Abbey.

1822   October. Abbey sold to John Farquhar. Christie's sale
        cancelled.
        Moved to Great Pulteney Street, then Lansdown Crescent, Bath.

1823   September 9 - October 29. Phillips' thirty-seven day sale at
        Fonthill Abbey.

1825   December 21. Fall of the Abbey's central tower.

1826   Embattled Gateway built.
        September. Building of Beckford's Tower began.

1827   Spring. Exterior of the Tower completed.

1828   Early August. Virtually ignored death in London of Franchi,
        his friend for forty years.

1834   January 27. Birth of Henry, first of seven great-grandchildren
        born in his lifetime.
        June. *Italy; with Sketches of Spain and Portugal* published.

1835   June. *Recollections of an Excursion to the Monasteries of
        Alcobaça and Batalha* published.

1844   February. Intended publication date of *Views of Lansdown
        Tower, Bath.*
        May 2. Died at Lansdown Crescent, Bath.

Watercolour of Beckford's Tower from the west by W. H. Bartlett, 1829.

The Tower

No doubt William Beckford had plans for building a tower at Bath even before he moved there from Fonthill Abbey in 1822. A correspondent to a London evening paper wrote in October the following year, 'Beckford has just bought Lansdown Hill which is the scene of the most active labours, and the summit is being prepared for the erection of a Saxon tower'. Beckford justified the choice to a friend by describing the view from Lansdown as 'the finest prospect in Europe'. It was at about this time that he commissioned a young local architect, Henry Edmund Goodridge, to design a tower for him.

Although a Saxon tower (for which drawings survive) was originally proposed, the final design derived from other sources, notably Stuart and Revett's *Antiquities of Athens* (1762), a work Beckford had in his library. In style the square shaft of the 120 foot Tower is austerely Italianate, with distinct echoes of the unfinished campanile of Verona Cathedral, while the octagonal lantern rising above its stonework was inspired by both the Choragic Monument of Lysicrates and the Tower of the Winds at Athens.

Goodridge engaged John Vaughan of Bathwick to build the Tower, and the stone was quarried nearby. Work began early in 1826, and the Tower shaft itself was speedily erected between the end of that September and the beginning of November, when the lower cornice was reached. John Buckler's drawings in the British Library, dated April 1827, show that masonry work on the entire building had been substantially finished by then. Goodridge used gilded cast iron for the cupola and the eight columns of the lantern which was otherwise made entirely of wood. The two-storey building at the base of the Tower housed many of Beckford's treasures although he never intended to live there. It was a retreat to which he could retire to contemplate, or to study his rare books and manuscripts.

As it was in Beckford's time, the main entrance is on the north side of the Tower through the three-arched loggia to the vaulted passage. However, the arrangement of the rooms and even their number has changed more than once since then. In his day, having reached the vaulted passage, you turned left for the ground floor. On the right was the Vestibule, small but nevertheless splendidly decorated in scarlet and purple. At the far end was a door to the garden, planted by Beckford with rare trees, while an opening on the right led into the principal room on the ground floor, the Scarlet Drawing Room. Here he kept some of his finest china in heavy carved oak cabinets on either side of the bow window; possibly these cabinets and some of the other pieces of furniture in the Tower were designed by him in conjunction with Goodridge. Beneath the windows now overlooking the cemetery stood a table whose top was a large slab of Egyptian granite. On his daily visit to the Tower from his house in Lansdown Crescent, Beckford took great pride in arranging flowers in a vase on this table.

The Spiral Staircase leading to the Belvidere.

The Crimson Drawing Room by Willes Maddox, from Edmund English, **Views of Lansdown Tower, Bath,** *1844.*

Back in the vaulted passage another door led to the single-storey annex containing a kitchen and perhaps a bedroom for Beckford's occasional use with a narrow closet between the two. This housed a pump handle connected by a rod through the floor to a cylindrical lead pump in the basement. Water was drawn from a well which also received rain water from the roof. A tunnel below the loggia runs from this basement to the original central heating furnace under the Tower itself, from which warm air rose to heat the shaft and, it was once thought, through ducts within the Tower walls to heat the Belvidere (as spelt in Beckford's time) as well.

At the opposite end of the vaulted passage the fine circular staircase with 154 steps, formerly carpeted, ascends to the Belvidere. After climbing for a complete turn to the first storey, there is a platform in the centre of the stairwell where a very large vase of Peterhead granite ornamented with bronze used to stand. As well as providing a dramatic focus, the vase also served as a conduit for the Tower's warm air heating system. At this level a door led to the Sanctuary, a narrow room dominated by a marble statue by Rossi, now in Lisbon, of Saint Anthony of Padua, Beckford's adopted patron saint. A subdued light would have been provided by glass domes set into the roof.

Next to the Sanctuary was the Crimson Drawing Room whose size and furnishings were similar to those of the Scarlet Drawing Room below. The coffered ceilings of these drawing rooms contained crimson or scarlet panels richly decorated with gilt cornices. Beckford reserved the Crimson Drawing Room for many of the treasures kept at the Tower, including objets d'art depicted in three oil paintings by Willes Maddox which are now on display. A door in the far left corner led to the Small Library with an ornate barrel-vaulted ceiling. Next to this, but entered from the stairs via a lobby, was the Etruscan Library with bookcases ingeniously supporting a false ceiling. The display of books here was said to be so dazzling that visitors were less ready to leave this

Objets de Vertu No.1. Oil painting by Willes Maddox, c.1844. (Tower Collection).

room than any other.

Continuing up the stairs, and passing a door to the flat roof of the two-storey building, the Belvidere is reached. From here the panoramic view is magnificent on a clear day. The twelve plate glass windows could be opened by sliding them upwards into apertures in the wall – the four central sashes to a greater extent than the others. All the windows in the two-storey building had iron lattices on the outside which gave them an Oriental character while also protecting the works of art from attempted burglary, and the lattices were echoed by the heavy iron balustrades for the Belvidere windows. The ornate ceiling of this room is the only one to survive even partially intact and, after two major restorations, has been reconstructed mostly using evidence from Willes Maddox's lithograph of 1844.

Fifty-three wooden steps, not accessible to the public, wind up from the centre of the Belvidere to a platform just below the cast iron cupola. Halfway up there is an octagonal gallery lit by glazed vertical slits and at the very top a range of timber windows masked by ornate gilded bulls-eye grilles look out from each side.

In 1830, the future Queen Victoria came to Bath with her mother, the Duchess of Kent. Before visiting Bath Park, which the Duchess requested be called Royal Victoria Bath Park, the party went to Beckford's Tower. Although contemporary reports do not say so, presumably Princess Victoria was among those present. What she thought of the Tower was, sadly, not recorded as she did not begin her famous journal until 1832.

Some of the contents of the building were sold in a two-day sale in 1841, after which the rooms were refurnished. How they must then have looked can be gathered from the colourful lithographs in a large folio work, *Views of Lansdown Tower, Bath*, intended for publication in February 1844, although it did not appear until later in the year. However, a few months before this, Beckford died. He had hoped to be buried next to his dog near the Tower but his family was unable to have the land consecrated, so his granite sarcophagus had to be moved from there to the newly opened Bath Abbey Cemetery at Lyncombe. Goodridge designed cast iron railings and stone piers to surround the tomb, and the railings were so impressive that the Coalbrookdale Company, who made them, showed a section at the 1851 Great Exhibition.

Beckford probably had a hand in their design as they incorporate cinquefoils and crosses flory, both motifs proclaiming illustrious ancestors on his mother's side. Her father was a member of the

Objets de Vertu No.2. Oil painting by Willes Maddox, c.1844. (Tower Collection).

The Belvidere today, looking very much as it did in Beckford's time.

ancient family of Hamilton which was represented by the cinquefoil, while through her mother he could trace a direct line back to the first Lord Latimer, whose coat of arms was a gold cross flory on a red field. Soon after work started on the building of Fonthill Abbey in 1796, he began to use these motifs on the backs of some of his books and elsewhere. It was appropriate that they should finally be used on the railings for his tomb. Beckford left the Tower and its contents to his daughter Susan, wife of the tenth Duke of Hamilton. The greatest treasures and all the books were removed to Hamilton Palace in Scotland, but she sold the Tower and the remaining contents in November 1845. Most Beckford sales attracted a great deal of attention and this one was no exception, with even the *Illustrated London News* reporting it over several issues containing many views of the rooms and objets d'art.

At this sale the Tower failed to reach its reserve, and in 1847 was sold with an acre of land for a mere £1000 to a local publican who proceeded to turn it into a beer garden. When the Duchess of Hamilton

heard about this, she asked Goodridge to buy back the Tower from the publican regardless of expense, and he parted with it for an extra £731 which included the solicitor's fees. Having regained possession, she gave the Tower and grounds to Her Majesty's Commissioners for Building New Churches for use as a cemetery, on condition that her father's body was removed to it and that the railings and piers round his tomb at the Abbey Cemetery were incorporated in the entrance to the new cemetery. The Rector of Walcot, the Rev. Sidney Herbert Widdrington, who had officiated at Beckford's funeral and was under the mistaken impression that the ownership of the Tower had been transferred to him, paid for the cemetery to be laid out. He commissioned Goodridge to design the Byzantine entrance gateway, and the railings and piers were duly erected on either side of it.

After the ground floor had been converted into a funeral chapel, with an altar in front of the bow window at the west end and a new doorway cut through to the vaulted passage, the chapel and grounds were consecrated by the Bishop of Bath and Wells in April 1848. Previously he had refused to allow Beckford to be buried there, but now it was possible for his body to be reburied at the spot he had chosen close to the Tower, although his dog had to be dug up first. The tomb, commissioned in Beckford's lifetime was, at his daughter's suggestion, isolated from the other graves by an oval ditch to keep people away. There have been rumours that the land on which it stands was never consecrated, but they are unfounded. Perhaps they arose because

Beckford's tomb in Bath Abbey Cemetery, from **Illustrated London News,** *29th August 1846.*

Beckford's Tower from the south-east showing the gateway to the cemetery on the right. Carte de visite, c.1870, by J & J Dutton, Bath.

Beckford was buried above ground, but this was the custom in Saxon times and he claimed descent from the Saxon kings. Possibly this also explains the earlier reference to a 'Saxon' tower; Beckford may initially have meant the Tower to be simply his mausoleum rather than the treasure house it became.

Goodridge died in 1864 and was buried quite close to Beckford. In the same year the then Rector of Walcot paid for some repairs to the Tower stonework which cost £100 and in 1884 he spent a similar sum on the upper part of the Tower. He made it clear that future rectors must not feel obliged to follow his example and that he had paid for the work himself because the Tower was such a prominent feature of the neighbourhood. The Bath publisher Peach, writing in 1888, commented unfavourably on this second restoration. He thought that as the building had cost the parish nothing, they might at least have kept it in good condition.

Urgent repairs to the Tower were again necessary by 1898 when donations were sought. For the next three years damaged masonry was replaced and the roofs of the lower part of the building repaired under the direction of Goodridge's son. However, he failed to stop the leaks and could only partially correct the tilt. Neglected maintenance during the First World War prompted an observer to write in 1918, 'the tower is piteous in its abandonment: here a heavy open-work shutter in gilt-bronze wrenched off its hinges, there a gilt-bronze medallion fallen to the ground; the stripped walls scrawled with graffiti, the

ceilings dilapidated and the rain beating in'.

One morning late in February 1931 a mysterious fire spread through the two-storey building, destroying panelling, decorations and ceilings that were very much as Beckford had left them. A defective flue may have caused the fire which also blackened the walls of the circular staircase. A few days later the Rector of Walcot launched an appeal for the complete renovation of the building. By 1934 the chapel had been enlarged and restored, being given a tunnel-vaulted ceiling nearly two storeys in height. It now occupied all the space previously taken by the Scarlet Drawing Room, the Vestibule, the Sanctuary, and the Crimson Drawing Room.

For some time the Tower's stairs had been considered unsafe and the fire made matters worse. Over the years the rusty handrail had become insecure and some of the Regency cast iron balusters detached. In Beckford's lifetime those wishing to see the Tower had to apply to his factor for tickets and, except during the Second World War when being used by the Women's Voluntary Services during the day and the Home Guard at night as an observation post, it was usually open to the public. By 1954 it was considered dangerous and was closed.

Walcot Parochial Church Council then appealed for funds, chiefly to repair the lantern and renew the staircase handrail. Their architect's survey revealed that water had decayed the oak collar on which the eight iron columns of the lantern rested, causing the whole lantern to settle southward, a defect endemic from the day the cast iron columns were erected in 1827 (coach screws securing their bases had been driven through the lead covering which should have been protecting the timber from incoming water). Water had also damaged the ceiling and floor of the Belvidere. A donation by Dr and Mrs L. T. Hilliard in 1957 (in memory of her father who was buried in the cemetery and had been interested in Beckford) enabled some modest external repairs to the lantern to be completed. The stairs, however, were still dangerous to use as insufficient funds were raised to finish the internal repairs.

Efforts were made throughout the 1960s to secure the Tower's future. Then, the Pastoral Measure of 1968 enabled the Church Commissioners to sell redundant churches, and in the following year the Rector of Walcot asked the diocesan authorities in Wells for permission to sell the Tower. He said, 'It has neither ancient value nor contemporary interest: it's not even a good folly'. Admittedly it was a rather damp and cold funeral chapel that was simply a liability to the parish, and at this point Dr and Mrs Hilliard offered to buy it.

In 1970 the Church Commissioners declared the cemetery chapel redundant. After Bath City Council had granted planning permission for a change of use from a place of worship to a dwelling house, the Church Commissioners invited offers which had to be accompanied by a brief description of any proposed alterations to the building. Several offers were received, and in May 1971 the scheme prepared by Dr. and Mrs. Hilliard was the one accepted. The detailed specification and plans for this were drawn up by J. Owen Williams, their building surveyor. When the draft redundancy scheme had been sealed by the Church Commissioners and confirmed by the Privy Council, the freehold was transferred to the Hilliards in January 1972 for £5000. That June, they launched Beckford's Tower Restoration Fund.

Much renovation work was then undertaken. A drawing by Goodridge, which he presented to the Institute of British Architects in 1836, shows a terrace with stone steps leading up to the main entrance from the original gravel drive. These steps

Dr & Mrs Hilliard in 1972, during the restoration of the Tower's entrance steps to the north.

and wall, which were removed when a sloping approach to the chapel was made for funerals, were rebuilt to restore their original appearance. The circular staircase in the Tower was given a new handrail, and specially cast balusters were fitted to replace those missing. The top of the Tower was repainted and weatherproofing improved; the Belvidere plasterwork was partially restored, as far as a limited budget would allow.

By the spring of 1973 two flats had been created, with the larger one, called Beckford House, occupying the two-storey building. Four new windows were skilfully inserted in the south façade to match the original ones, and a new first floor was constructed to replace that lost in the fire. The single-storey annex contained the much smaller Beckford Flat, with new stairs leading down to a basement room. Here, the semi-lunar window had been hidden behind an earth bank which was removed to restore it to the original design. Now, for the first time in almost twenty years, the Tower could again be visited by the public.

Soon after the Hilliards had established the Beckford Tower Trust in January 1977, a north-facing bedroom on the first floor was converted into a museum. That autumn it became the Lansdown Room, devoted to Beckford's time in Bath, while the doorway from the circular staircase to the sitting room of Beckford House was reopened to create a second museum room, the Fonthill Room, overlooking the cemetery.

For many years the old cottage by the road was the home of successive caretakers of the cemetery, although it existed before the Tower was built. It is shown in T. H. Shepherd's drawing of the Tower from the north in 1829 and at one time Beckford's gardener James Vincent lived there. When the cottage was vacated it fell into serious disrepair and, like the Tower, it had been damaged by vandals. It was structurally improved and remodelled, and given the name Beckford Cottage. A new drive was made from Lansdown Road, beside the cottage, and a car park formed in front of the Tower. A strip of land towards the water tower on the west was bought from Bath Corporation and landscaped.

Restoration 1997-2000

When in July 1994 the area under the floor of the Belvidere was examined, a steel beam inserted during the 1931 restoration was found to be badly rusted, forcing open joints in the surrounding stonework. It was later discovered that steel used elsewhere had caused similar damage, and that one of the cast iron decorative window grills in the Belvidere was in danger of falling through the roof of the museum below. As well as the extensive corrosion found in the ironwork, the survey confirmed the continuing decay in the lantern's timberwork. Urgent repairs were proposed early in 1995 and the Beckford Tower Trust applied for Lottery funds through English Heritage.

By April 1996 the application had been accepted and that October planning permission for the repairs was granted. Soon afterwards the Heritage Lottery Fund offered a grant; this required the Trust to find matching funds for which an appeal was launched in April 1997. By December 1999 the projected total cost of the restoration had reached £650 000, of which £462 500 was met by the Heritage Lottery Fund. A public appeal and the resources of Bath Preservation Trust and the Beckford Tower Trust raised the matching funds.

The builders, Emerys of Bath, began preparatory work on the Tower in October 1997, at which time the restoration was expected to take a year. Once the scaffolding had been erected, the architect, archaeologist and engineer could begin recording

Repaired ring beam from the lantern using secondhand Douglas Fir and sound original wood, August 1998.

how the upper stages had been constructed and then altered over the years. At the same time a building historian was commissioned to report on the history of the Tower by tracking down relevant archives in local and national collections.

Initially it had been hoped that only a partial dismantling of the lantern would be needed, namely the removal of the cast iron roof panels and eight columns, and also the timber infilling panels and the lead-lined gutterwork around the base of the lantern; this would leave the skeleton framework of the main timbers exposed for inspection and repair. It soon became clear that the decay of the original timber framing had spread throughout the main uprights and that the damp had encouraged beetle infestation hidden at the time of an initial survey of the lantern's condition by a thick layer of bird and fly droppings.

There was no alternative but to dismantle all of the structure affected. As this proceeded, it was found that the lantern's wooden framework had been poorly constructed or indifferently repaired in an effort to correct the tilt. Instead of timbers being properly mortised together, four- or six-inch spikes

Dismantling the cast iron roof of the lantern for restoration, February 1998.

Detail of gilded cast iron lantern roof.

had been used to reinforce joints. Some of the timbers were short pieces butt-joined together rather than whole lengths. The tensioning system of iron rods originally designed to keep the framework in place had also failed, and repairs had been made that appeared to do more harm than good. The only solution was to rebuild the entire frame using existing timbers where possible, and at the same time introducing a stainless steel system of anchoring and tensioning the whole structure down to a network of beams inserted just above the Belvidere ceiling.

Because of the Tower's very exposed position, a watchful eye will always have to be kept on it in the future. Wind which might seem mild at ground level can well reach gale force at the top, forcing rain through the minutest gaps in the structure.

While the restoration of timber and masonry proceeded on the site, Dorothea Restorations of Bristol removed the dismantled cast iron roof panels, columns and balustrade panels to their workshops for shot-blasting and repainting. The decision to re-gild was taken because traces of gold were found under layers of paint, confirming contemporary accounts of the glittering appearance of the lantern.

Four of the eight columns proved to have been poorly cast with numerous blow-holes which had to be filled before their conservation could begin. During the 1931 restoration, the ring of iron acanthus leaves round the rim of the roof had been removed, because many had fallen off and no money was available from the Walcot Parish funds to

replace them. Fortunately there was a single survivor and a mould was made from it, enabling the entire ring to be replaced. Most of the scroll-shaped ornaments to the ribs between the eight roof panels had also fallen off and new castings were made to replace them.

Re-gilding was carried out in draught-free conditions using books of ultra-thin 23.5 carat English gold leaf, the purest available, supplied by the last gold beaters in the country. The ironwork, which had been treated with a hard-wearing epoxy resin paint, was coated with glue size; when it became tacky the gold leaf was applied with a flat brush which had been lightly flicked across the gilder's cheek to take on a minute amount of oil and static. Any overlapping gold was then removed with a clean brush.

Research among plaster pieces excavated from the original heating chamber at the foot of the staircase, together with Willes Maddox's lithograph of the Belvidere, enabled its ceiling to be re-created. In the 1970s, restoration, it had only been possible to repair part of the circular frieze and the decorative spandrels. Now the centre of the ceiling is once more

Beckford's Tower today, from the east.

Books from Beckford's Library showing cinquefoils and crosses flory.

The Tower Today

Visitors to the Tower today, as well as admiring the view from the Belvidere, can see exhibits in the two museum rooms on the first floor. Here, displays interpreting Beckford's life and his years at Fonthill, his home until he was over sixty, can be seen in the room formed from his two libraries. His final years in

Chinese Armorial Porcelain Plate. Ch'ien Lung, c.1755. Probably made for Alderman Beckford, William's father. (Tower Collection).

coffered within rings of egg-and-dart moulding, and the walls and ceiling are painted in the 1844 colour scheme, as revealed through paint analysis. The Trust also commissioned the re-creation of the Belvidere's original eight buff worsted damask curtains lined with scarlet serge and bordered with silk lace, along with the X-framed stools. Today the Belvidere appears very much as it was in Beckford's time. The restoration of the Tower was commended in 2001 with a Civic Trust Award and in 2002 by the Royal Fine Art Commission Trust's Building of the Year Award for Restoration.

In 1999 the Landmark Trust took a sixty-year lease on the ground floor rooms. The Scarlet Drawing Room has again become a living room, now splendidly decorated to evoke Beckford's rich interior. The Vestibule contains the kitchen, while there are two bedrooms and a bathroom in the single-storey annex. People in search of an unusual holiday home can rent this spectacular flat and ascend to the Belvidere to contemplate the world beneath them, as Beckford used to do.

Bath are explored in the adjoining room which it is hoped will eventually be redivided into the Crimson Drawing Room and Sanctuary, and re-created in the style depicted in Willes Maddox's colour lithographs published in 1844. The lantern can now be floodlit, creating an ethereal night-time vision.

Most of Beckford's treasures are now privately owned or dispersed in museums and art galleries throughout the world. Brodick Castle on the Isle of Arran and Charlecote Park, Warwickshire, contain fine collections of his furniture, ceramics and precious objects, and nineteen paintings formerly owned by him are in the National Gallery in London. In America, New York's Metropolitan, the Huntington in California, and the National Gallery of Art in Washington have paintings from his collection. Beckford's personal archive, including unpublished manuscripts and many letters to and from him, is in the Bodleian Library, Oxford. Yale University's Beinecke Library also has a substantial holding of Beckford material.

Six Silver Gilt Spoons. George III, 1790s. The two on the left are engraved with the cross flory and the others with Beckford's crest. (Tower Collection).

Lansdown Cemetery

In Victorian times Lansdown Cemetery was an important final resting place for Bath notables, but it had become rather overgrown of late, and the restoration of the Tower provided an incentive to improve the cemetery's appearance. This work has been greatly helped by very generous private donations and a financial initiative between the Beckford Tower Trust and Bath & North East Somerset Council, and supported by Walcot Parish. As well as the graves of Beckford and his architect, Henry Edmund Goodridge, other impressive tombs in the cemetery are those of Sir William Holburne, founder of the Holburne Museum in Bath, and James Wilson, a prolific local architect. Work began on clearing the area in 1997, and paths following the original lines of the graves were cut, enabling a start to be made on cataloguing the graves in the following spring.

Goodridge's handsome entrance gateway was repaired and cleaned in 1999, the intention being to

Goodridge's entrance gateway to the cemetery (1848).

re-establish it as the principal entrance to both cemetery and Tower. Both sides of the area in front of the Tower and parts of the higher ground next to the water tower are planted using species mentioned by Beckford, or ones that he would have known. The railings along the boundary wall by the road, except for the two curved quadrants, were removed during the last war for salvage. Through the generosity of the J.M.R. Charitable Trust many improvements were made to the cemetery and the missing railings were replaced. They were cast by the Scottish ironfounders, Ballantine Boness Iron Co, using as a pattern the surviving curved railings which, a paint analysis has revealed, were originally dark green.

Coalbrookdale railings at the cemetery entrance, formerly around Beckford's tomb.

William Beckford by Joshua Reynolds, 1782. By courtesy of the National Portrait Gallery, London.

William Beckford

William Thomas Beckford was born on 29th September 1760 at Soho Square, London. His father, Alderman William Beckford, was twice Lord Mayor of London and is largely remembered today for standing up to George III who gave a curt reply to an address that the Alderman had presented to him.

Beckford's father died when he was nearly ten, and so great was his inheritance that Byron called him 'England's Wealthiest Son'. This enormous fortune came from sugar plantations in Jamaica developed by earlier generations of the Beckford family.

In spite of this great wealth, Beckford was a man of considerable taste, and during his long life he amassed a fine library and collections of pictures, furniture and objets d'art. Beckford's estate was at Fonthill, in a region of fertile downland fifteen miles west of Salisbury and here, after his father's death, he spent a spoilt and luxurious youth. He also travelled widely on the Continent and in his old age published edited diaries of his journeys.

The Alderman's seat, Fonthill House, known as Fonthill Splendens because of its opulence, was a handsome Palladian mansion built in 1755 soon after the previous house had been burnt to the ground. Here Beckford was taught by tutors as his mother did not wish to send him away to school, and

Fonthill House (known as Splendens), Wiltshire, seen from the east across the lake, by Hendrik de Cort, c.1791. By kind permission of the Trustees, Sudeley Castle.

this rather solitary existence allowed Beckford's mind to wander in many directions. When he was eighteen he visited his distant cousin William 'Kitty' Courtenay at Powderham Castle in Devon, starting a friendship that may not have been entirely platonic. Certainly rumours were spread and it was a scandal that Beckford never wholly lived down.

He published in 1780 a slim volume, *Biographical Memoirs of Extraordinary Painters*, an amusing account of the lives of six fictitious painters with names like Watersouchy of Amsterdam. The housekeeper at Fonthill gave visitors so much false information about the paintings that he thought a little more would surely do no harm.

In the following year Beckford held a coming-of-age party on a fantastic scale. All the local people were invited, and feasting and other activities went on for several days. That Christmas there was an even more lavish party for a select group of friends in the specially decorated house. One of the guests was Louisa, wife of his cousin Peter Beckford (author of *Thoughts on Foxhunting*). For some time she had been using her charms, partly in an attempt to diminish Beckford's interest in Kitty.

Inevitably Beckford went on the Grand Tour and while abroad he kept a diary of experiences and impressions which formed the basis of *Dreams, Waking Thoughts, and Incidents*. This was printed in 1783 but on the eve of publication was suppressed by his family who thought that it was too unrestrained a book from one destined for a political career. In the next year he had himself elected Member of Parliament for Wells and later for Hindon but, finding the business of the House dull, resigned after ten years.

During this time Beckford had been studying oriental manuscripts and books which inspired him to produce his own Arabian tale, *Vathek*. He wrote it in French and it was much admired by Byron, who said, '*Vathek* bears such marks of originality, that those who have visited the East will have some difficulty in believing it to be more than a translation'.

In 1783, before *Vathek* was published, Beckford married Lady Margaret Gordon who two years later bore him a daughter, Margaret. A second daughter Susan, was born in Switzerland in 1786, but Lady Margaret died a few days later. Her death was a blow from which he never recovered and thereafter he lived the life of a recluse. A further blow was the publication of *Vathek* without his permission by his friend, also his cousin's tutor, the Rev. Samuel Henley, to whom he had entrusted the manuscript for him to translate into English. Not only was Beckford's name not mentioned, but Henley gratuitously suggested that the manuscript was obtained from a man of letters in the East. This first edition of 1786 has been followed by many others and it remains in print today.

The next ten years Beckford spent quietly either at Fonthill or travelling abroad. To escape from the Wiltshire gentry who would have nothing to do with him, he thought of settling in Portugal where he had many friends. One was Gregorio Franchi, a seventeen year old boy who became the most

Susan and Margaret Beckford by George Romney, 1789. The Henry E. Huntingdon Library and Art Gallery, San Marino, California.

*Fonthill Abbey. View of the West and North Fronts after John Martin, from John Rutter, **Delineations of Fonthill and its Abbey**, 1823.*

important figure in his life at Fonthill. As well as managing the Abbey, Franchi helped him to buy and design objets de vertu. During this time he began to think about building a retreat on high ground about a mile from his mansion. He commissioned the architect James Wyatt to design a Gothic summer-house and in the latter half of 1796 building began. Curious villagers from Fonthill Gifford were unable to inspect the new works as Beckford, before leaving on a visit to Portugal, had given orders that a twelve-foot-high wall of over four miles in length be built round part of the Fonthill domain. This was intended to keep out huntsmen rather than prying locals; Beckford loved all forms of wildlife and strongly objected to horses and dogs trampling over his land in pursuit of their quarry.

By 1800, the summer-house was rapidly assuming the form of a Gothic Abbey inspired by the monastery at Batalha in Portugal. The Abbey consisted of southern and western wings meeting under a spire which collapsed and was replaced by a tower. This in turn had to be rebuilt a few years later in stone as it had been too hastily constructed in wood and plaster.

That Christmas, Nelson, accompanied by Sir William and Lady Hamilton, stayed with Beckford and an evening trip to the Abbey was the highlight of the visit. One of the many anecdotes about Beckford relates that he was driving Nelson at high speed through his grounds in a four-horse phaeton when he sensed some anxiety on the part of his guest. Presently Nelson said, 'This is too much for

Fonthill Abbey. Interior of St Michael's Gallery, from John Rutter, **Delineations of Fonthill and its Abbey**, *1823.*

me. You must set me down', whereupon the intrepid national hero descended and together they walked back to the house.

By the middle of 1801 building at the Abbey had progressed enough for Beckford to consider living there, although it was not until 1807, when Fonthill Splendens was largely demolished, that he finally moved in. The main entrance was through thirty-five-foot-high doors into the west wing, a vast baronial hall. Beckford satisfied his love of contrast by having these great doors opened and shut by a dwarf whom he rescued from miserable circumstances in Italy. Broad steps led from here up to the centre of the building, the Octagon, above which rose the two-hundred-and-eighty-foot tower. To the north lay King Edward's Gallery, enriched with stained glass and plaster coats of arms of Beckford's ancestors who were Knights of the Garter. Among the magnificent furniture was a large table, beautifully inlaid with marble and precious stones, from the Borghese Palace in Rome and now

at Charlecote Park, near Stratford-on-Avon.

Beyond this gallery was the Oratory, dimly lit by lancet windows. On an altar stood the statue of Saint Anthony of Padua, later to be the focal point of the Sanctuary in Beckford's Tower at Bath. St Michael's Gallery ran south from the Octagon and it, too, was sumptuously furnished. There were numerous smaller rooms of equal magnificence.

Although Beckford seldom entertained, he led a busy life at Fonthill. He supervised the building of the Abbey, and the landscaping of the grounds by his gardener, Vincent. Also there were frequent parcels of new books from London dealers for him to examine.

In 1810 Beckford's younger daughter Susan married the Marquess of Douglas who later became the tenth Duke of Hamilton. Beckford entirely approved of the match but was less pleased when, in the following year, his elder daughter Margaret eloped with and married Colonel Orde, a man of small estate and limited prospects compared with those of Susan's husband. This caused an estrangement between Beckford and Margaret that lasted until just before her early death in 1818.

Wyatt was killed in 1813 when his coach overturned and Beckford must have received the news with mixed feelings. Although Wyatt created for him a fantastic Gothic Abbey, he was a frustrating architect to employ. Often he failed to arrive when expected, causing irritating delays for the quick-tempered Beckford. Luckily most of the Abbey had been completed by then but the grandiose east wing, containing several hastily constructed drawing and dining rooms, was never properly finished. He intended it to commemorate his descent from all the barons (of whom any issue remained) who signed the Magna Carta.

While Beckford was living at the Abbey, his sugar estates in the West Indies were badly managed and his income from them dwindled. The building of the Abbey had considerably reduced his capital and in 1822 he decided the time had come to live on a more modest scale. Christie's were instructed to sell the Abbey and most of the contents. For the first time the Abbey was on view and people flocked to see it from all over the country. Over seven

Lansdown Crescent, Bath, showing Beckford's bridge.

thousand catalogues were sold at a guinea each, but before the sale began the entire property, except for the best third of the contents which Beckford kept, was sold for £300 000 to a rich and somewhat eccentric Scottish merchant, John Farquhar.

Beckford then moved to Bath where he would have liked to buy Prior Park, but the price was too high for him. After the first few months, he moved to 20 Lansdown Crescent, buying also 1 Lansdown Place West which he later sold after he had built the bridge connecting the two houses. He subsequently bought 19 Lansdown Crescent to keep his neighbours at a distance. Here Goodridge created a library for him and covered over the stairs to the first floor so that Beckford could ascend them unwatched by passing servants.

He acquired a strip of land immediately to the west of Lansdown Road between his houses and the Tower, where the faithful Vincent laid out a ride. In 1826, to form a barrier between his garden and the more open land to the north, Beckford built an embattled gateway bearing an ancient coat of arms to which he had no claim. It can still be seen today in the garden of a house in Lansdown Road. The ride led up the hill, passing through plantations with suitably placed benches from which to admire the view. If Beckford decided that some ground should be turfed or planted with shrubs, it had to be done at once. As at Fonthill, Vincent was usually able to gratify these whims even if it meant working through the night. Approaching the Tower, the ride descended briefly into a grotto tunnel, now mostly filled in, to avoid crossing a road to a farm. Beyond lay the Tower Garden, planted with exotic trees and shrubs. (In 1985 Beckford's Ride was listed Grade II in English Heritage's Provisional Register of Parks and Gardens of Special Historic Interest.)

Meanwhile, the new owner of Fonthill Abbey held a sale in September 1823. Beckford could now buy back more books and pictures, avoiding the many lots misleadingly sold by the auctioneer, Phillips, as having come 'from Fonthill Abbey'. Two years later the central tower of the Abbey collapsed owing to inadequate foundations, demolishing most of the west wing, but luckily without injuring anyone. Cyrus Redding, Beckford's first biographer, originated the often repeated legend that Beckford noticed its absence from the view next day when visiting his unfinished Tower. Work on the shaft had not begun by December 1825 when the tower of the Abbey, 25.3 miles away, fell. However, the Abbey's tower was 930 feet above sea level while Lansdown Hill is 750 feet high, and no hills between are high enough to obstruct the view, so the legend may possibly be true.

The Embattled Gateway by Willes Maddox, from Edmund English, **Views of Lansdown Tower, Bath,** *1844.*

Farquhar sold the Abbey ruins and estate early in 1826 and died a few months afterwards. Many of the nearby farms and cottages have a door or a piece of stained glass taken by local residents from the

Abbey, and what they left was pulled down in 1846 except for the northernmost fragment which still stands today.

The twenty-two years that Beckford lived in Bath were years of almost total retirement, but sometimes he was to be seen riding through the streets of the city with his retinue. He kept in close touch with the Duke and Duchess of Hamilton and was very proud of their children. In his last years he also had five great-grandchildren. He continued to travel, mainly to London to consult booksellers and picture dealers. Above all he read his books, writing copious remarks in them on their merits or failings.

By no means all Beckford's treasures were in the Tower. The two houses in Lansdown Crescent were full of costly furniture, pictures and books which were greatly admired by his occasional visitors. Among other old masters, there were paintings by Titian, Raphael and Canaletto, drawings by Rubens and engravings by Rembrandt and Durer. Gustav Waagen wrote in 1838, 'I shall never forget the dining-room, which, taken all in all, is perhaps one of the most beautiful in the world'.

Eventually the diaries of his European travels were published. *Italy; with Sketches of Spain and Portugal* appeared in 1834 and *Recollections of an Excursion to the Monasteries of Alcobaça and Batalha* in the next year. Both were highly praised by contemporary journals. Beckford would not allow his *Episodes of Vathek* to be published in spite of Byron's request to see them, and they did not appear until 1912.

After a brief illness, Beckford died on 2nd May 1844 at the age of 83. A few days previously he had summoned his daughter who came from Hamilton Palace to be at his bedside. The simplicity of the deathbed shown in Maddox's painting was in sharp contrast to his funeral, the most splendid ever seen in Bath. A local newspaper reported that twenty thousand people lined the route to the Abbey Cemetery to watch the cortege.

Beckford was notable in many roles: writer, collector, patron of the arts, traveller, landscape gardener and architect. As the sum of these parts, he emerges as one of the most fascinating men of his time.

Medal cabinet in oak inlaid with ebony and parcel gilt, made for William Beckford, probably after a design by H E Goodridge, c.1837-41. (Tower Collection).

Bibliography

FIRST EDITIONS OF BECKFORD'S WORKS

Biographical Memoirs of Extraordinary Painters, 1780.

Dreams, Waking Thoughts, and Incidents, 1783, but suppressed on the eve of publication.

An Arabian Tale [Vathek], 1786.

Modern Novel Writing, or the Elegant Enthusiast, 1796 [1795].

Azemia, 1797.

Al Raoui, 1799. Sometimes attributed to Beckford.

A Dialogue in the Shades, etc., 1819. Attributed to Beckford.

Epitaphs, some of which have appeared in the Literary Gazette of March and April, 1823. [1825.]

Italy; with Sketches of Spain and Portugal, 1834.

Recollections of an Excursion to the Monasteries of Alcobaça and Batalha, 1835.

The Episodes of Vathek. Translated by Sir Frank Marzials, 1912.

The Vision and *Liber Veritatis*. Edited by Guy Chapman, 1930.

The Journal of William Beckford in Portugal and Spain 1787-1788. Edited by Boyd Alexander, 1954.

Life at Fonthill 1807-1822. From the Correspondence of William Beckford. Translated from the Italian and edited by Boyd Alexander, 1957.

Beckford's 1794 Journal. Edited by Boyd Alexander in *William Beckford of Fonthill*, Howard B. Gotlieb, Yale, 1960.

The Beckford Edition. Beckford's music, edited by Maxwell Steer, 1999.

The Consummate Collector: William Beckford's Letters to His Bookseller. Edited by Robert J. Gemmett, 2000.

BIOGRAPHIES OF BECKFORD

Cyrus Redding, *Memoirs of William Beckford*, 2 vols., 1859.

Lewis Melville, *The Life and Letters of William Beckford*, 1910.

J. W. Oliver, *The Life of William Beckford*, 1932.

Guy Chapman, *Beckford*, 1937.

H. A. N. Brockman, *The Caliph of Fonthill*, 1956.

James Lees-Milne, *William Beckford*, 1976.

Brian Fothergill, *Beckford of Fonthill*, 1979.

Timothy Mowl, *William Beckford: Composing for Mozart*, 1998.

OTHER BOOKS RELATING TO BECKFORD

James Storer, *A Description of Fonthill Abbey*, 1812.

John Rutter, *Delineations of Fonthill and its Abbey*, 1823.

John Britton, *Graphical and Literary Illustrations of Fonthill Abbey*, 1823.

Edmund English, *Views of Lansdown Tower, Bath*, illustrated by Willes Maddox, 1844.

William Gregory, ed., *The Beckford Family*, 1887. 2nd ed., much enlarged, 1898.

Henry Venn Lansdown, *Recollections of the Late William Beckford*, 1893.

Marcel May, *La Jeunesse de William Beckford et la Genèse de son 'Vathek'*, 1928.

Guy Chapman & John Hodgkin, *A Bibliography of William Beckford of Fonthill*, 1930.

Sacheverell Sitwell, *Beckford and Beckfordism*, 1930.

André Parreaux, *William Beckford, Auteur de Vathek*, 1960.

Fatma Moussa Mahmoud, ed., *William Beckford … Bicentenary Essays*, 1960.

Boyd Alexander, *England's Wealthiest Son*, 1962.

Robert J. Gemmett, *William Beckford*, 1977.

Maria Pires, *William Beckford e Portugal*, 1987.

Devendra Varma, ed., *The Transient Gleam: A Bouquet of Beckford's Poesy*, 1991.

Didier Girard, *William Beckford, Terroriste au Palais de la Raison*, 1993.

Malcolm Jack, *William Beckford. An English Fidalgo*, 1996
[1997].

Jon Millington, compiler, *Beckford and His Circle in the
Gentleman's Magazine*, 2001.

EXHIBITION CATALOGUES

Howard B. Gotlieb, *William Beckford of Fonthill* (Yale
University Library), 1960.

Peter Summers, *William Beckford* (Holburne Museum,
Bath), 1966.

William Beckford Exhibition 1976 (Salisbury and Bath),
1976.

Malcolm Baker et al., *Beckford and Hamilton Silver from
Brodick Castle* (Spink, London), 1980.

William Beckford & Portugal (Queluz, Portugal), 1987. In
Portuguese and English.

Argenteries: Le Trésor du National Trust for Scotland
(Brussels), 1992. In French and Flemish.

Jon Millington, *Souvenirs of Fonthill Abbey* (Beckford's
Tower), 1994.

Derek Ostergard, ed., *William Beckford 1760-1844:
An Eye for the Magnificent*
(New York and London), 2001.

**Places to visit in the UK associated with William
Beckford and his collection**

Barber Institute of Fine Arts, University of Birmingham
British Museum, London
Brodick Castle, Isle of Arran, Scotland
Charlecote Park, Warwickshire
Dyrham Park, Gloucestershire
Fitzwilliam Museum, Cambridge
Gilbert Collection, Somerset House, London
Glasgow Museums, Glasgow
Guildhall, London
Holburne Museum of Art, Bath
Kingston Lacy, Dorset
Lennoxlove, Haddington, Scotland
Lord Mayor's Chapel, Bristol
National Galleries of Scotland, Edinburgh
National Gallery, London
National Portrait Gallery, London
Salford Art Gallery, Greater Manchester
Stourhead, Wiltshire
Tate Gallery, London
Upton House, Oxfordshire
Victoria & Albert Museum, London
Wallace Collection, London

A Website giving information on the latest
developments at both the Tower and Cemetery can be
visited at:
www.bath-preservation-trust.org.uk

Another Website devoted to William Beckford is at:
http://beckford.c18.net/beckfordiana.html

There is a Beckford Society, whose Secretary is
Sidney Blackmore,
15 Healey Street,
London NW1 8SR.

The Landmark Trust at Beckford's Tower
Bookings for the Beckford Tower apartment (suitable for
four people) are made with The Landmark Trust. For
further details, please telephone 01628 825925.
www.landmarktrust.co.uk

ACKNOWLEDGEMENTS

Published by Bath Preservation Trust

Printed by Colour Graphics, Bath

Photography:-

Alex Ramsay / Country Life Picture Gallery:
Page 8   The Belvidere.

A Currie / Beckford Tower Trust:
Page 11   Tower restoration.

James O Davies:
Titlepage Beckford's Tower Lantern by night.
Page 12   Beckford's Tower today.

Mandy Reynolds, ABIPP, Fotoforum:
Page 13   Chinese Armorial Plate.
Page 14   Six Silver Gilt spoons.

Jon Millington:
Page 13   Books from Beckford's Library.

Pat Millington:
Page 20   Lansdown Crescent.

7th Edition July 2002.

Many thanks to Sidney Blackmore, David Machin, Jesca Verdon-Smith and Theo Williams for all their help.

ISBN 1 898954 90 9

Opposite:
Plan of Beckford's Tower, showing room arrangements c. 1844.

Back cover:
Beckford's Tower from the east (detail). Sepia drawing by H V Lansdown, c.1855. **Victoria Art Gallery, Bath & North East Somerset Council.**

I. BECKFORD.	XVI. SCOT.
II. HAMILTON.	XVII. SCOTLAND.
III. LESLY.	XVIII. SAXON KINGS.
IV. ABERNETHY.	XIX. WALTHEOF.
V. ROSS.	XX. ALDRED.
VI. COMYN.	XXI. KEVELIOC.
VII. QUINCY.	XXII. GERNONS.
VIII. BELLOMONT.	XXIII. MESCHINES.
IX. MELLENT.	XXIV. LUPUS.
X. GWADYR.	XXV. ALGAR.
XI. FITZ OSBORNE.	XXVI. CAITHNESS.
XII. YVERY.	XXVII. DOUGLAS of Dalkeith.
XIII. GRANTESMESNIL.	XXVIII. READING.
XIV. GALLOWAY.	XXIX. COWARD.
XV. MORVILLE.	XXX. HALL.

Scheme of thirty quarterings registered at the College of Arms in 1808 by William Beckford.
© The College of Arms, London, MS. Norfolk 2, p.176.